Circles

Prayers for the End of Life

Fayegail Mandell Bisaccia

Weaverbird Press

Weaverbird Press
PO Box 688
Ashland, OR 97520
541-482-5565
888-804-7787
orders@weaverbirdpress.com
www.weaverbirdpress.com

Nautilus photo © Stockbyte / SuperStock
Portrait by Shianna Walker

ISBN 978-0-9789122-1-5

For Allness

Contents

One ⁊ **Bereaved**
For C.R. in memory of K.H.

Sacred Source, please.
Bring me a moment's respite all throughout the day.

Help me see the sunrise through the granite-dust-filled air.
Help the stricken gods regain their vision and then guide and
walk with me through mountain shadows.

Bless me with the courage to go on
without my most belov'd companion,
yet embraced by those who care—
in this time, in this place, in this empty house.

Bring solace in my memories
and help the sea sound soothe me
as I wander in the wilderness of this new world.

Sacred Source, please.
Bring me a moment's respite all throughout the day.

Two ❧ Open Window

Allness

Breath has ceased.
I know what to do.

Close his eyes, open the window, light the candle.
But what, really?
What does it mean? I sit at the edge of Mystery.

I peer with longing into the other realm.
I'd draw him back if I could.
No, not to this body claimed by cancer,
but to the sweetness of Life shared, touching Vastness.

Show me, Exquisite One, as I sit awed in Stillness,
what has changed?
I feel his presence in Your Presence.

I sit in Silence
awaiting my own return to

Allness.

Three ❧ Graveside Service

Author of Life—and Death

Today it is written. There is no going back.
No more hoping there has been a cruel mistake.

Prayers drone. Chants beseech You—grant him peace.
Sorrow drips from sodden trees and thunderheads loom ominous overhead.
Thunk. Red mud falls heavily on plain pine box.

This is it, Life Writer, Your last chance to change Your mind.
Won't You think about it one more time?
Is this the way the last act needs to end?
Ah, then comfort me, Creative One and

Teach me how to walk this fatherless path—
Fearless, with a peaceful heart.
There's no one else to guide me. Only You.

Now light Your candle.
Take up Your quill,

Author of Life.

Four ❧ *El Malei Rachamim*

Yes Beloved One

Lift up Your wings and shelter her,
Grant her peace, most Precious Gift.

You are our Source of Solace.
We stand weeping. It is we who need Your peace.
She now soars among the devas, takes her place with distant stars.

Yes, grant her perfect rest—if that is what she needs.
I question that. I think she'll go about her business,
Fascinated, wanting to explore that other realm
Where thinking makes it so and kindness is the modus operandi.

I pray for her excitement as she
Starts her new adventure, and I pray
She'll come and show me where she's been.

Yes, Beloved, shelter her and grant us peace.
You'll do what You want, I know,

Beloved One. I'll honor that.

Five ⌘ *Shiva*

My Comforter

Show me how to sit with loss
when I am yearning for her hug or loving touch.

Help me to believe she'll never make the bed
or brush her hair or cook our breakfast anymore.
No lighting candles for *Shabbat*, no *simcha*.

True, the evidence is there: black clothes and crowded livingroom
where people share their fondest memories. I cannot speak.
Their kindness overwhelms me. I withdraw.
The house is empty. You alone can comfort me.

Teach me to sit still and hold this pain.
"Sit still," the elders say. But all I want to do is pace,
cry out, retreat, or maybe disappear.

Show me how to find her in this deepest Void,
"Sit quietly," You say to me,

"and I will comfort you."

Six ❧ First *Yizkor*

Source of Grace

I bring myself to You this Day of Awe.
May *Torah* shine Her Light on all the seeking souls.

No easy day—this *Yom Kippur*.
A day for coming face to face with You,
Renewed. We've done our work.

We search for Grace in every supplication,
Finally assured that You and We are One.
But sometime in the midst of this
I find I must confront a scarier thing.

Soft music flows around my contemplation
And then the dreaded time draws near. Remembrance.
I hear a crowd of people leave the room. I am alone.

And then I lift my eyes and You are there in every face.
The room is filled with mourners of today and long ago.
Source of Grace, I shall survive. I know this now.

Seven ❧ Dedication

Gracious One

A year has passed.
No slick red clay today.

I walk with easier steps
As I approach this awesome border,
Gaze upon the slightly sunken ground, upon time passing.

A year has passed. I have survived
The stream of Holy Days that rocked me in my core.
Candles, *challah*, *kiddush* cup, placed before her empty chair,
A sign her Light remains.

I need no sign. You daily comfort me,
Stroke my tear-stained face
With wispy breezes, breath of Love.

I stand to face this gravestone.
A year has passed.

Gracious One, I stand in awe.

Eight ☙ Post Op

Blessed Healer

I sense Your Presence as I watch her
sleeping, wan, depleted, full of tubes.

I hold her hand in mine and trace her fingers,
stroke the knuckle wrinkles, nails, arthritic thumb.
The hands, so capable and full of life, lie still.

We talked about the surgery last night.
She had no fear.
She plans a speedy healing, full remission.
Source of Light, let it be so.

I hardly recognize her face without
the laughter in her eyes, her animated smile.
She's far from me. Is she with You?

Bring her back to me, Beloved.
Make her well again.

Healer, Blessed One, she's in Your hands.

Nine ⊰ Terminal Diagnosis

Holy One

As we sit shattered
help us find a way to take another step.

As we mouthe the biggest question, *Why?*
help us take our place among the many
who have walked this way before.

It is we who ask this question:
Sister, brother, daughter, wife.
There is no answer, this we know.
There is no answer, yet we search the Internet

search our souls search for simple fixes
complicated formulas life-destroying protocols.
Isn't this the one false diagnosis? Surely a mistake?

And finally we sit, shattered.
Calm us in this frantic time of disbelief

Holy Mysterious One.

Ten ☙ Hospice

Blessed One

As I embark upon this final journey,
give me courage to name what is true.

I started hospice today. I'm filled with ambivalence.
Tell me, is this a sign that Death is near, or the path to a richer Life?
Tell me, is this the "beginning of the end," or an exquisite opportunity?

Only You know that, Beloved.
Give me vision to see beyond my daily concerns.
Help me recognize the perfect moment for letting go
of each sacred thing—my home, my family, my life.

Surrender me to the caring support
of social worker, chaplain, nurse.
Let it be a gift for us—my family and me—
a comfort when we don't know what to do.

Is this my ending time on earth, Beloved?
Give me courage to name what is true.

Blessed one, give me courage.

Eleven ⅋ What's Gone Well Today?

My Comforter

Calm my racing heart and
help me find a reason to go on.

This giant bed engulfs me.
Tubes attach, it seems, to every vein and orifice.
What's gone well today? Remind me.

Help me understand the buzzes, beeps and flashes.
Give me patience to remain alone
with scowling nurses, tired at shift's end.
Show me where my equanimity has gone and call it back.

The other bed is empty and
I slept last night—no pain from twelve to four.
The doctor says the tubes may go tomorrow.

Beloved, grant me peace.
I feel the ebb and flow of breath.

Is that enough?

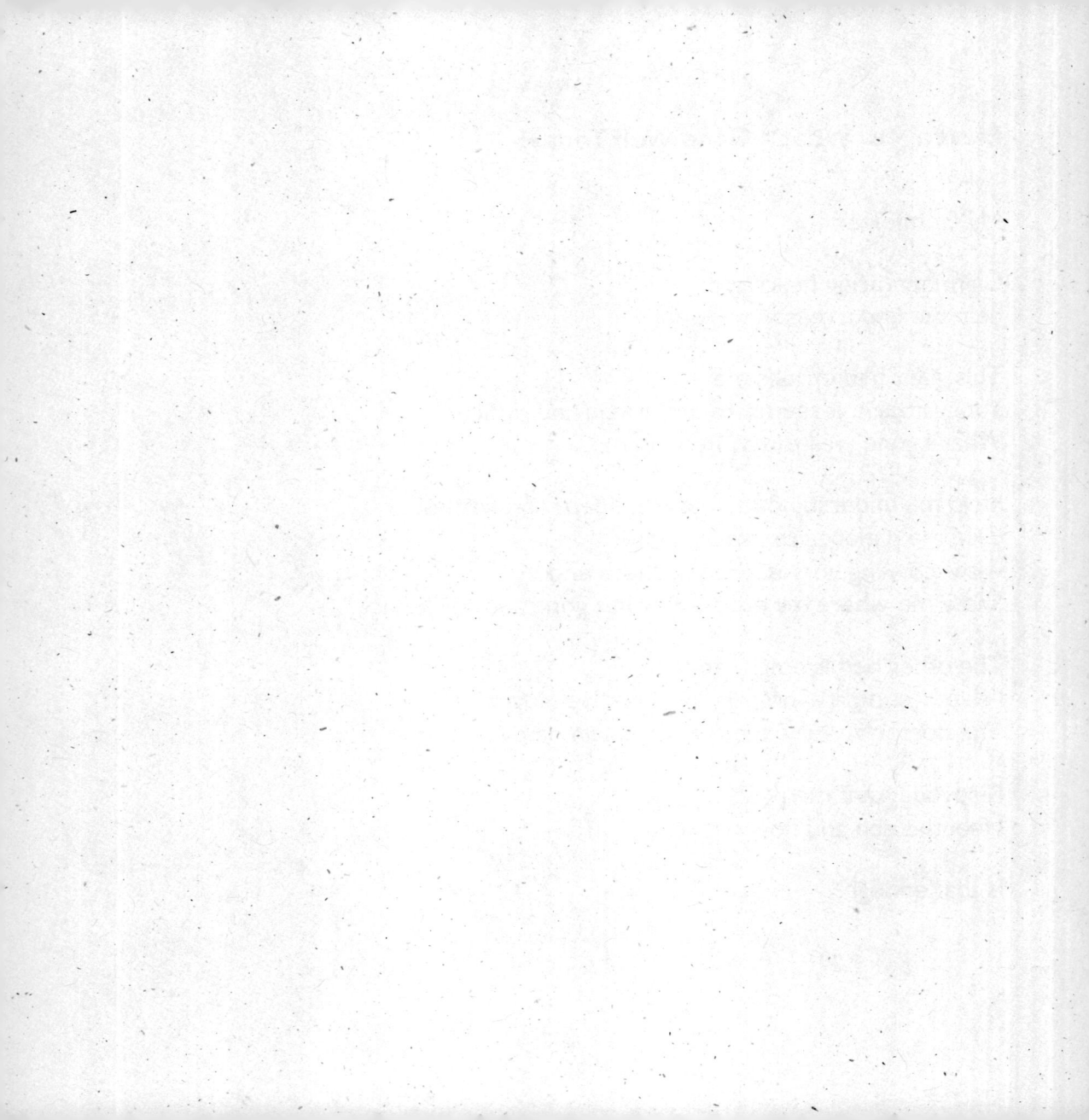

Twelve ⁓ Nausea

Source of All

Help me find You in this moment
right beside—within—the nausea that I feel.

It consumes me,
catches my attention,
holds me in its grip.

Is that where I must look for You,
in the Center of its center,
vast within the pin-point of this overpowering flood?
Show me how to find You.

Is it You I feel?
Are You calling me?
Will I find You, even here?

Beloved, give me peace with this intensity.
Help me feel the sweetness of Your Light.

Source of All, embrace me.

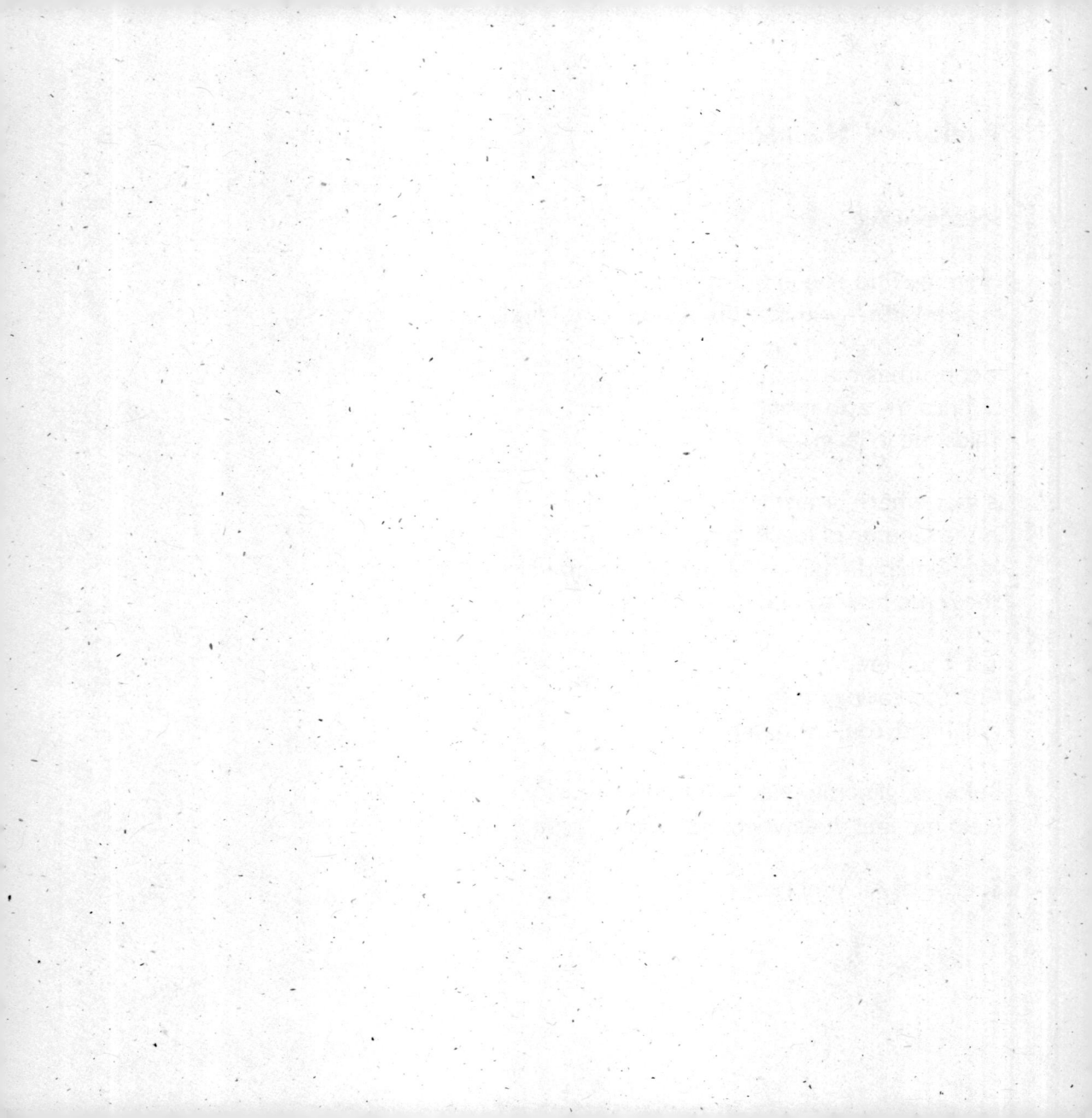

Thirteen ☕ Oxygen

Breath of Life, come close to me.

I hear the rhythmic breath machine.
Oxygen fills my lungs with You.

Help me feel the ebb and flow of strength,
the momentary resting point when it all stops
and then begins again. Flow out, breathe in.

The momentary pause. Is this the last?
Breathe out. Pause. Breathe in. Pause.
Rest and puff. Rest and puff.
Still my spirit. Breathe with me.

Still my spirit until the last rich breath
enters my lungs and slowly ebbs away.
Help me celebrate this opportunity to live.

In. Out. In. Out.
Breathe me. Be close to me,

Breath of Life.

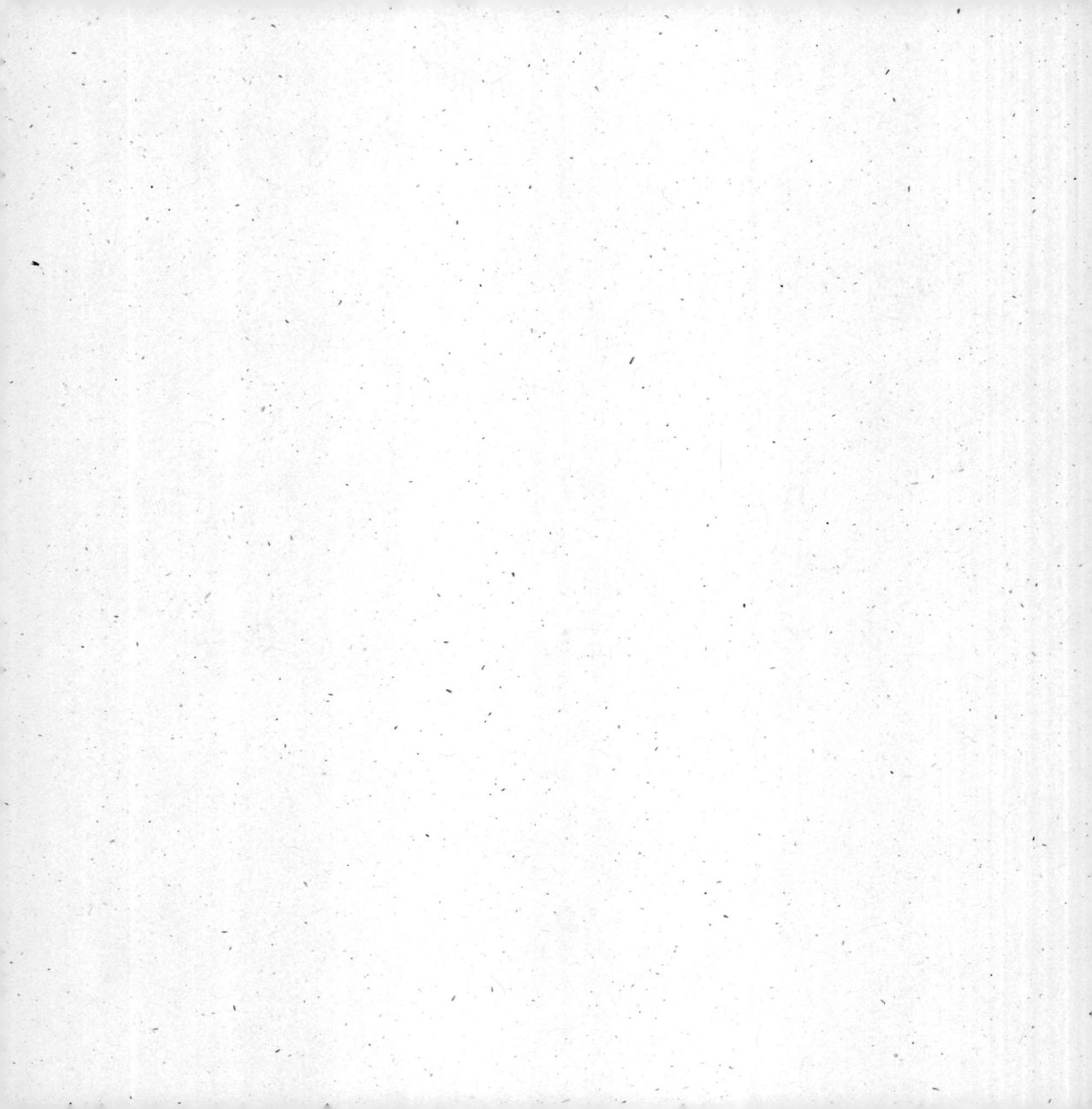

Fourteen ⌘ One Exquisite Thing

Source of Blessings Small and Large

I once lived with views of sunrise, birdsong, creek song, crickets, frogs.
It is time to hone my sensitivity.

Grant me Grace to find the beauty
here within four tiny walls. One small bed,
one cozy chair with handmade afghan
draped across my shaky knees.

Light and shadow are my playmates.
Help my spirit roam the hills, and then
I'll settle back content. Please help me find
the one exquisite thing about this moment.

Help me sense a loving touch, a gentle voice,
a real concern, a cup of tapioca made with Love.
My farthest destination? The commode beside my bed.

Help me hone my sensitivity on this journey Home.
My needs are meager, my wants are fewer still.

Remind me. Small blessings do suffice.

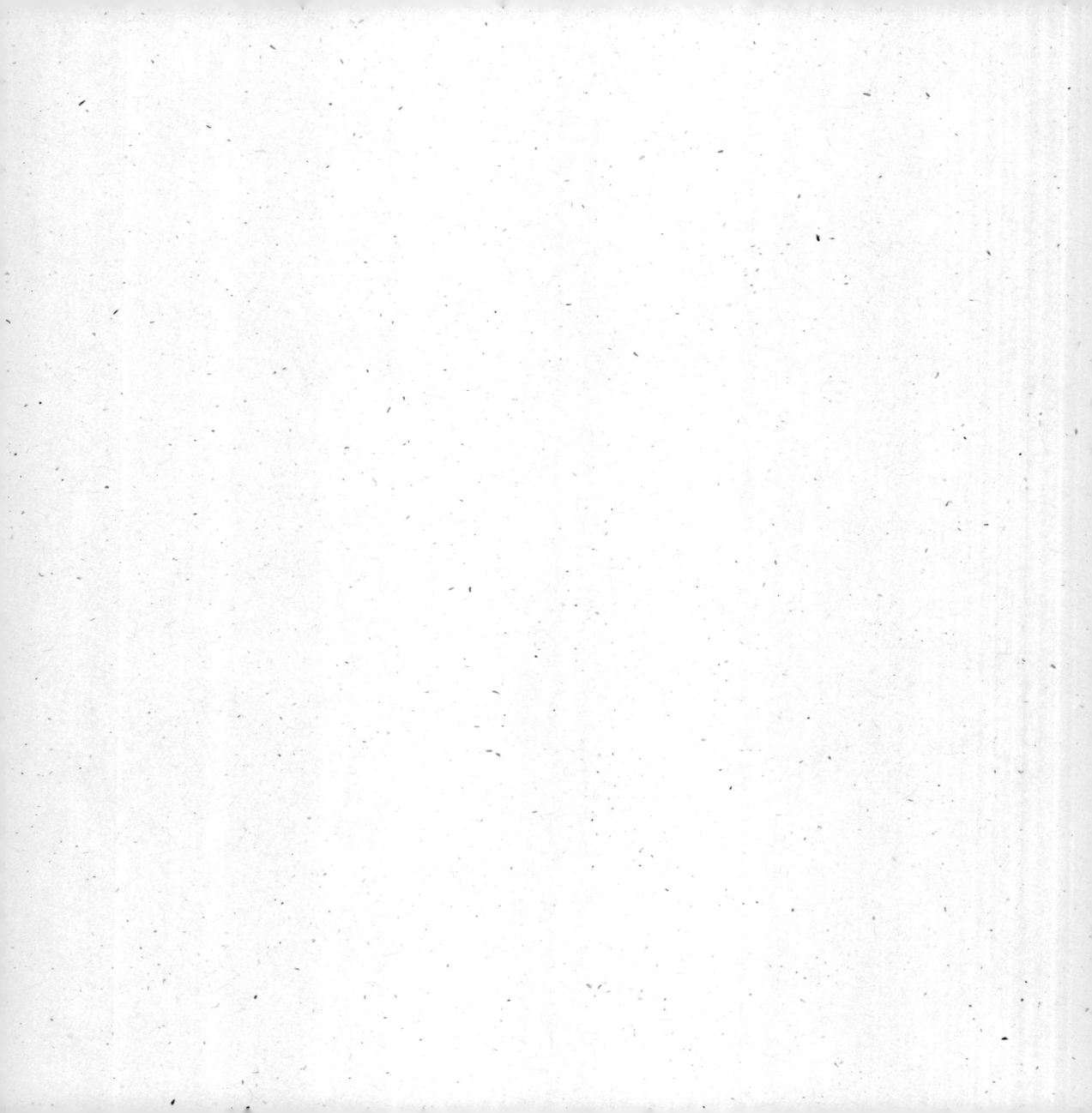

Fifteen ❧ **Bliss**

Source Within

Entice me with simplicity.
With You the worry slips aside

And in its place, a sweet serenity,
A roiling avalanche of Light,
A depth of Silence unbeknownst to me, 'til now.

All the days are filled with complications—
Things to solve and meds to try,
Broken hearts and broken dreams,
Distractions, all, from time with You, my Soul.

Clear away the clutter, Loving One.
When I but shift the focus from my thoughts
To You, all slides away, and I am left with

Sweet surrender into Bliss.
Away from time You carry me,

Dear Source Within.

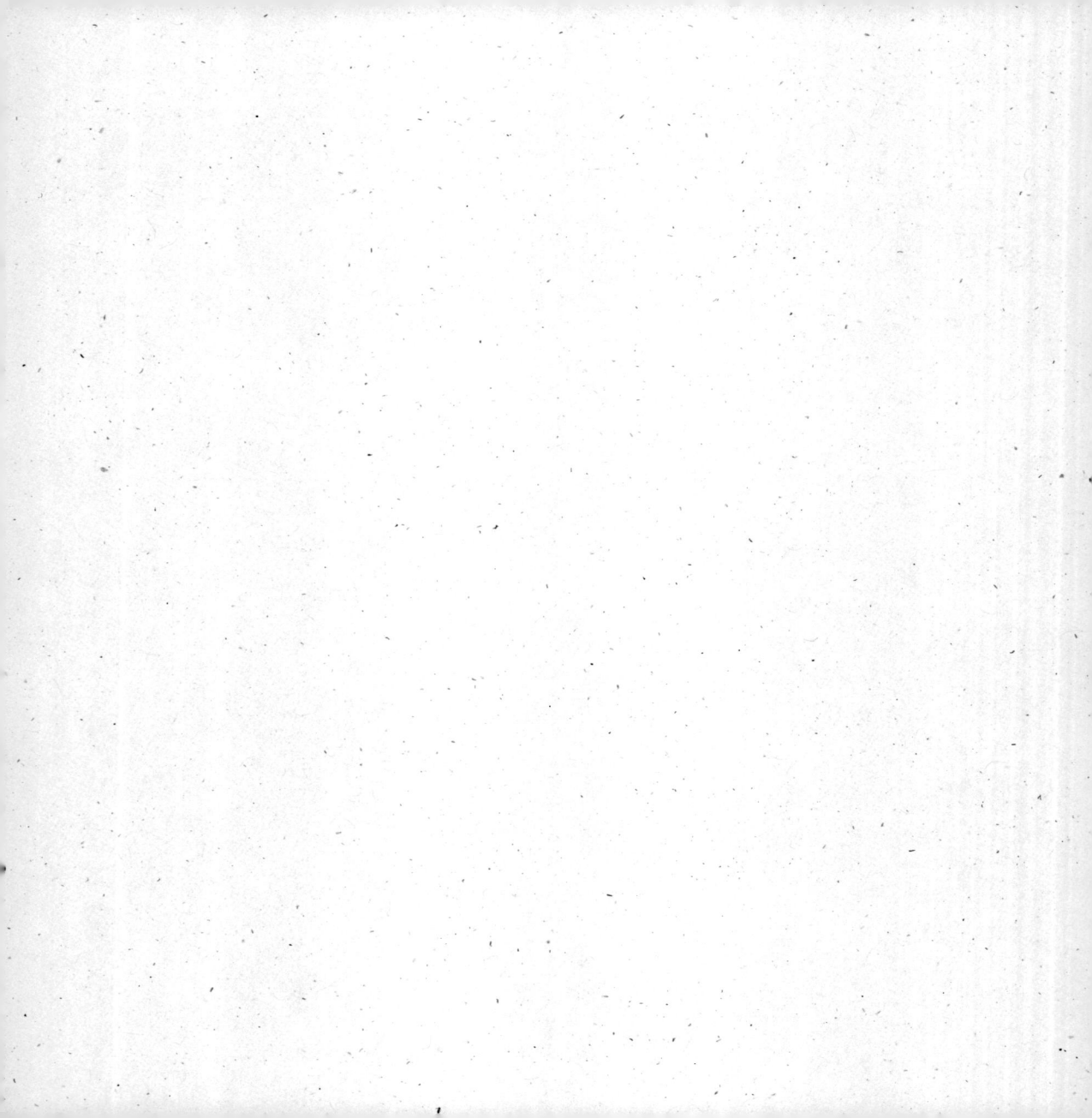

Sixteen ❧ Long Goodbyes

Compassionate One

We're in the season of the long goodbyes.
We've said the things we need to say

And yet this body lingers.
I wonder how it manages to stay alive.
Dearest, help me find perspective.

My family weeps with thoughts of empty rooms,
yet they will have each other when I'm gone.
Help us, Blessed One. We must remember.
I surrender everything and they surrender me.

This body lingers. Loved ones come, pay homage.
I recline in forest velvet gown.
They sit beside the bed and seek my wisdom.

I bless them with an aching heart
and wave goodbye, then nausea overwhelms me.

Compassionate One, help me weep, too.

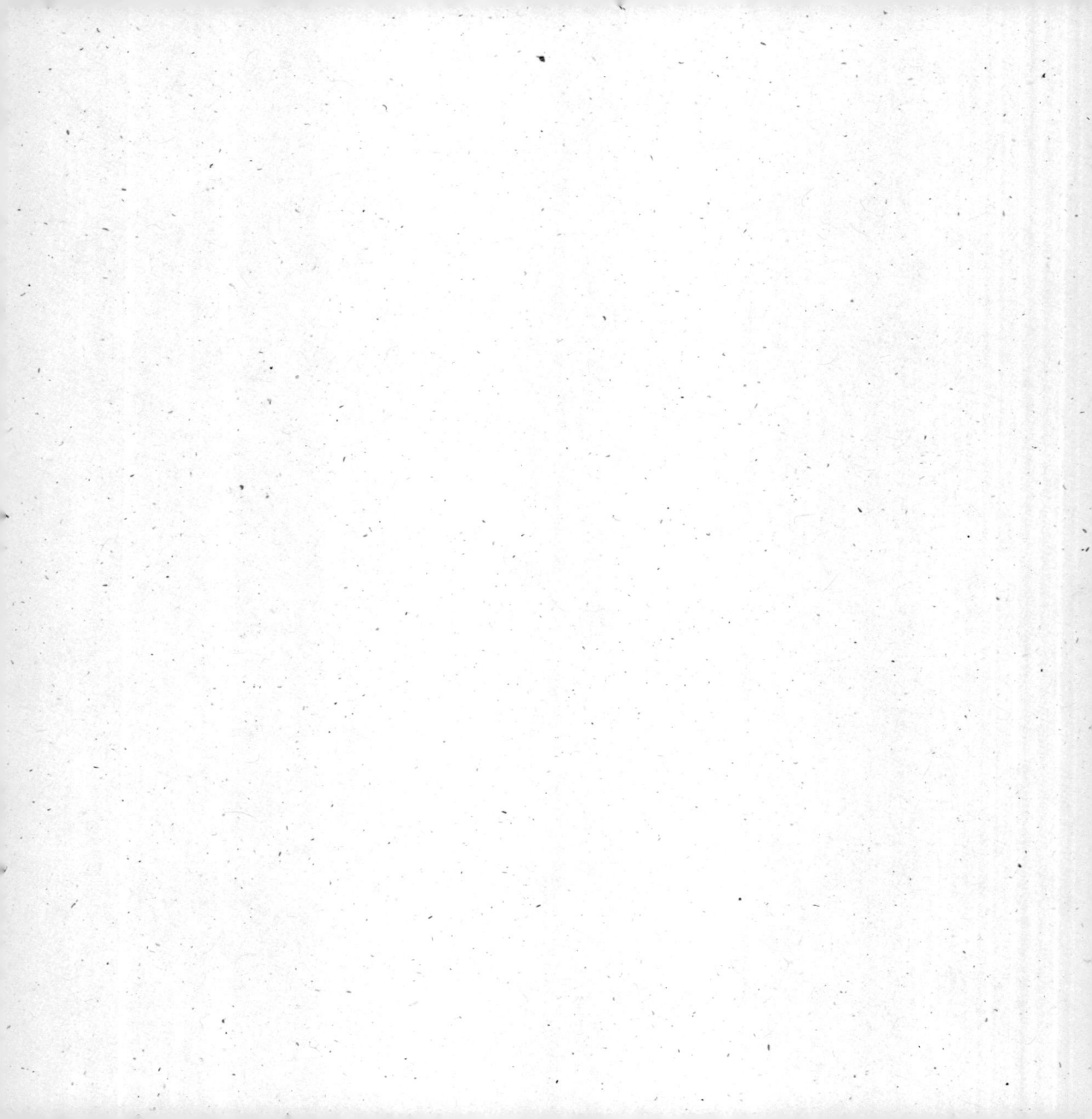

Seventeen ❧ *Viddui*

Source of Peace

Give me solace in these final hours, and patience.
Bring healing to those I leave behind.

I have searched my soul,
reviewed a thousand small mistakes,
and larger ones, of course.

I've made my peace with others and myself,
and now with You, All Love.
Is this my day to join You?
Only You know that.

I haven't felt like speaking much today.
Is this the time to say my last *Shema*,
proclaim Your Allness with my dying breath?

I'll take it as my final meditation, end-to-end.
Shema Yisrael YHVH [breathe in], *Eloheinu, YHVH* [breathe out], *echad.*

Source of Peace, that works for me.

*shema yisrael YHVH eloheinu YHVH echad shema yisrael YHVH
eloheinu YHVH echad shema yisrael YHVH eloheinu YHVH
echad.*

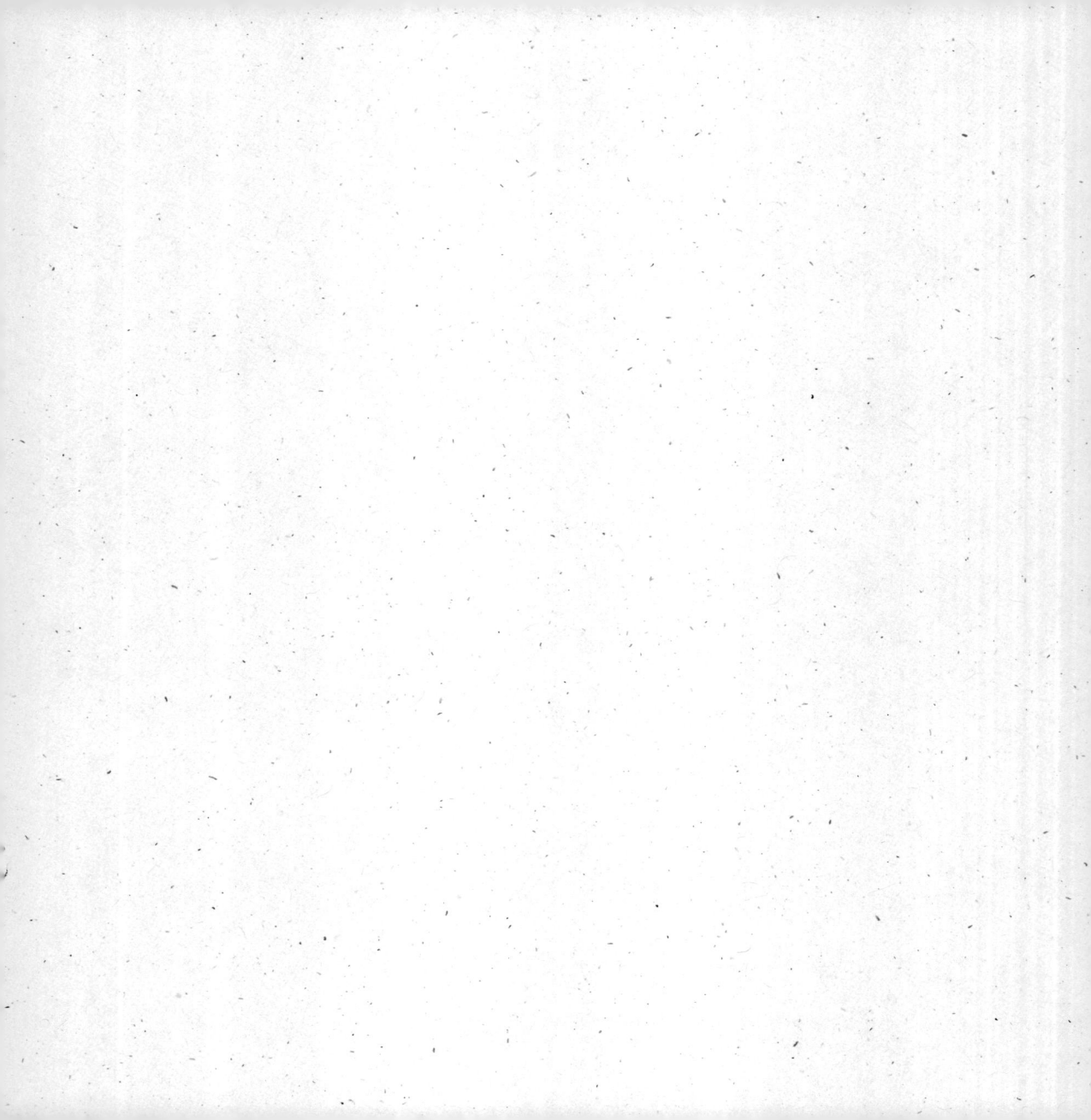

Eighteen ⌘ Vigil

For K.H. z"l

Blessed One

Move me freely
in this time of transition.

Rock me like a boat on crystalline sea.
Carry me on this river of Light
into Vastness, my new Home.

A silken sweetness comforts me
through words, through touch, through silence.
Help those who care for me bask, also,
in the endless sea of Love on which I float.

Take me as You've never done before.
As I set out upon this new adventure,
guide me lovingly.

I drift in different spaces, travel wide-eyed,
flow more deeply into Light.

Blessed One, move me freely in this time of transition.

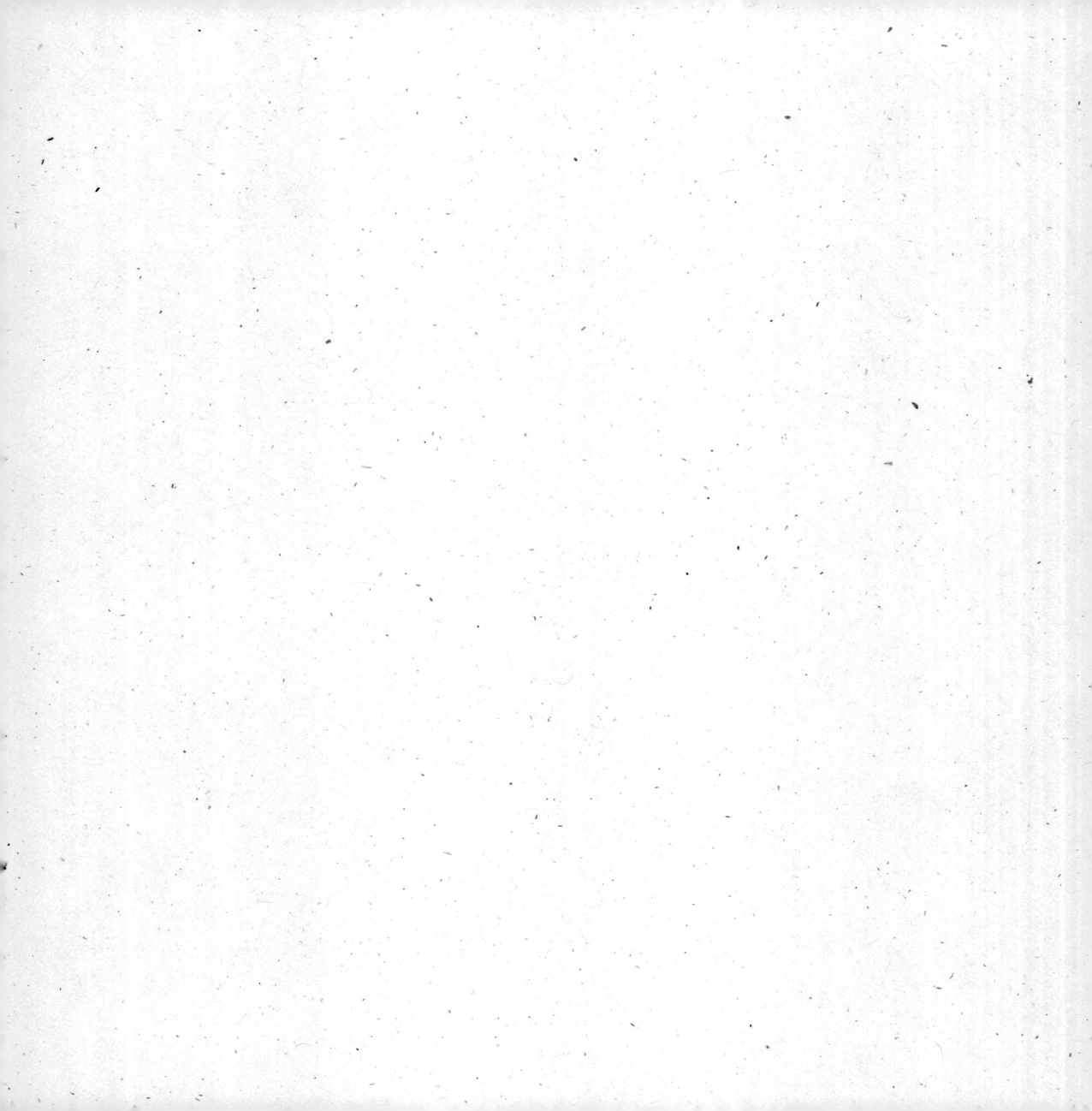

Dancing Lesson

Stillness.
Only Mother.
I am dancing.
She moves me as a breeze moves flame.
Quietly.
Her angel's fingers caress me.
She is gone six years and
she is present, vast, unbridled.
Vast.
She has no edges, only space.
Vast.
There is no Mother, only space.

I know her for her tenderness.
She brings no thoughts or guidance, no opinions.
And yet, she moves me.
I am sensing,
following her, with my body, with my being.
Sensing. And watching.

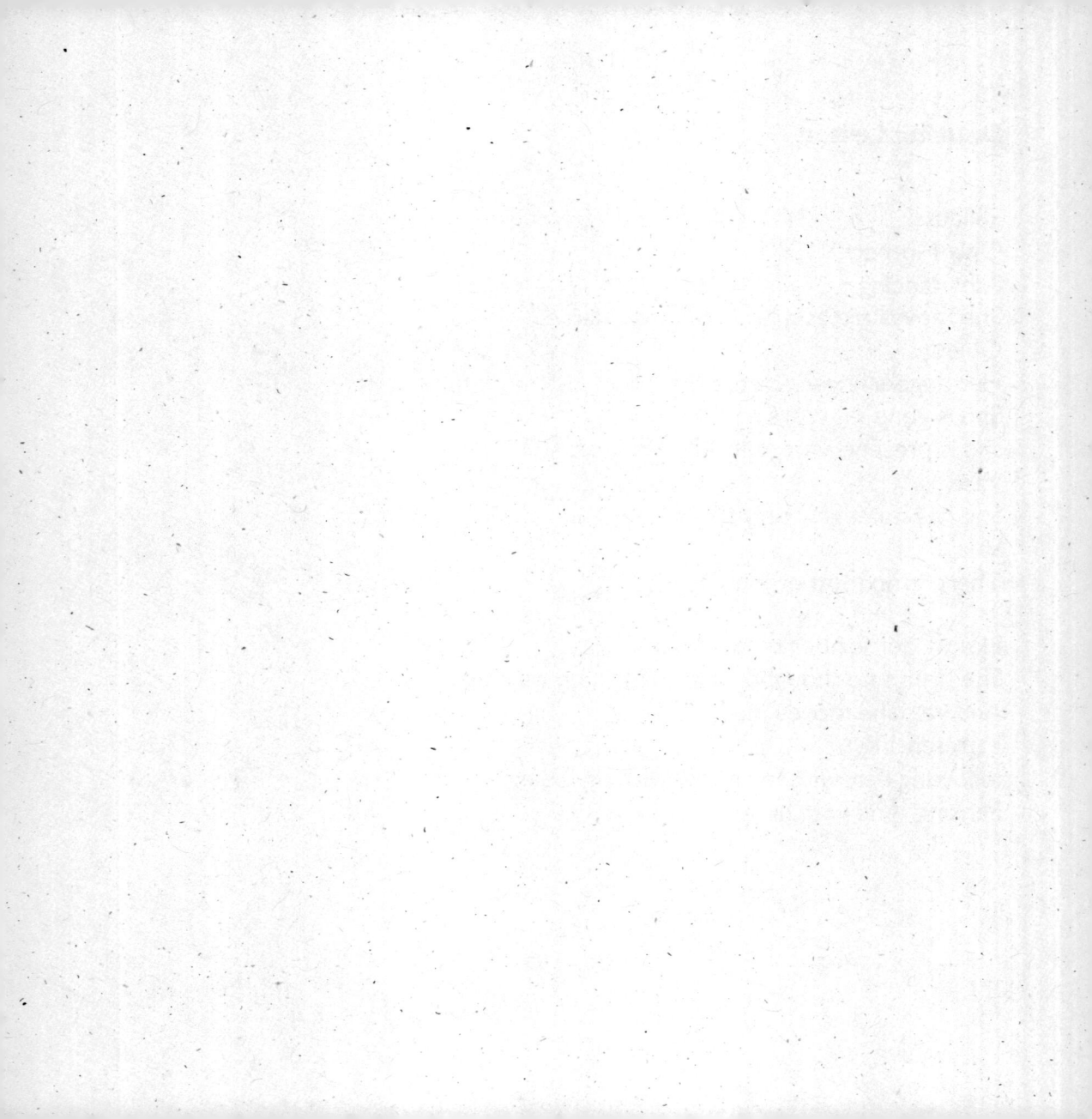

This I know:
Mother feels no pain.
She does not suffer.
She does not yearn for me.
She does not yearn,
she who is not she, but all.
Her vastness comforts me.

I am dancing,
deep in this place she has carried me.
I am purely present,
in no space,
in no time,
only in the music that is Mother's vastness.
No thinking,
no wanting,
only Mother.

Grief unfolds into movement
and escapes.

— From *Dancing in My Mother's Slippers*
by Fayegail Mandell Bisaccia

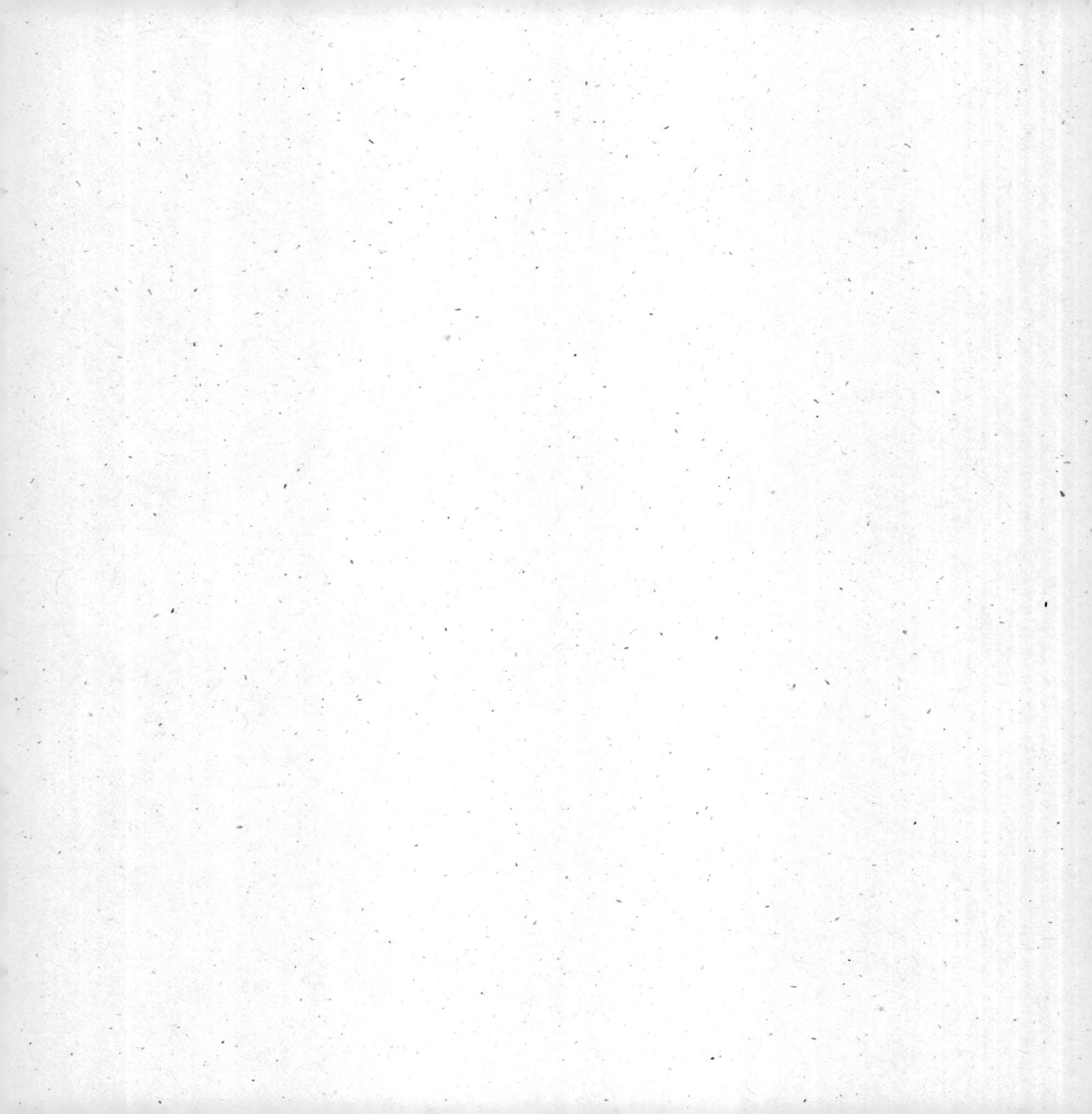